Yesterday's Rain
A Kid's Guide To Kauai, Hawaii

Photography by John D. Weigand
Poetry by Penelope Dyan

Bellissima Publishing, LLC
Jamul, California
www.bellissimapublishing.com

Copyright © 2013 by Penny D. Weigand and John D. Weigand

All rights reserved. No part of this book may be reproduced or transmitted in any form or by any means, electronic or mechanical, including photocopying, recording, or by any other means, or by any information or storage retrieval system, without permission from the publisher.

ISBN 978-1-61477-100-5
First Edition

"If a picture is worth a thousand words, then we should all take a hundred thousand pictures, and just sit silently in the Hawaiian sun."

PENELOPE DYAN

Yesterday's Rain
Bellissima Publishing, LLC

Introduction

There are tons of things for a kid to do and see in Kauai, Hawaii, and award winning author, attorney and former teacher, Penelope Dyan, along with photographer, John D. Weigand have combined their efforts once again to show you just a few of those things. You can kayak down a river, surf on the beach and you can see some fun and very beautiful birds. Chickens run wild on Kauai, surviving all on their own, left over from early settlers; and the Hawaiian geese are a real treat to watch, and they paddle right up to you. There is a lighthouse you can visit that is 100 years old, and it just had its birthday! And the color green is abundant, as the mist and rain caress the island daily. In fact, Mount Wai'ale'ale (near the center of the island) is 5,148 feet (1,569 m) above sea level. And it is said to be one of the wettest spots on earth, with an annual average rainfall of a grand total of 460 inches! Yes, you can go to a luau and eat out and do all those sorts of things; but you can also go bird watching, see a rainbow in a blowhole, and just lie under an umbrella on the beach and soak up the sun. This is why they call this place paradise! This book is also an early reader so a kid can practice reading skills though word recognition and rhyme, and there is a music video on the Bellissimavideo YouTube Channel that goes along with this book for more educational fun!

Yesterday's Rain
Bellissima Publishing, LLC

Yesterday's Rain
A Kid's Guide To Kauai, Hawaii

Photography by John D. Weigand
Poetry by Penelope Dyan

In Kauai there is so much to do!
You can sun on the the beach,
or you can play in the sand.
There is lots to do whether
on water or on land.
You can swim and go shopping
and there is much more!
From the harbor
you can hop aboard a trolley,
and travel inland from the shore!

You can see a waterfall,
and you can take a picture or two.
You can 'take a hike!'
It is all up to you.

You can drive right through what the Hawaiians fondly call 'the tunnel of trees.'

You can watch a white crane
sitting on a rock,
as you feel the trade wind breeze.

You can watch a mother hen gathering
her young hatchling brood around,
as she ruffles out her feathers
right there (in front of you)
on the parking lot ground!
She is their mother.
Each chick is her child.
And she takes care of each one
(all by herself)
because they are free. . .
and they roam in the wild.

And just when you think
there couldn't possibly be more,
you find a VERY mysterious cave,
and you decide to explore!

A 100 year old lighthouse
high above the ocean on a hill,
lights a path from water to land.
You imagine a pirate ship
from a far away sea,
making its way
through the rocks and the sand.

You can watch the surfers
ride the waves from the beach!
Or YOU can surf or swim!
In Kauai there's lots of stuff to do!
YOU won't know WHERE to begin!

Of course there are lots of shops
and places to eat,
where you can munch
on something extra sweet.
And the mist and the rain
hovers in the heavens high,
just waiting to join you
from up in the sky.
And as inconvenient as that may seem,
the rain comes to bring you
all the things that are green!

If you look closely you might also find,
a washing machine
of an old-fashioned kind.
It was once a modern convenience,
as everyone knows;
but it looks like it took a lot of work,
just to wash some dirty clothes!

There is a blowhole you can see
with a rainbow
that dances in the sun!
The water shoots right into the air!
It's LOTS of fun.
You can watch it spout and spurt
from day to night,
as the water plays
with the sun's reflecting light.

And then when your vacation is done,
and it is time to say aloha
to the sand and the sun,
there is only one more thing
you need to say,
and that is, "Mahalo!"
until another day.

"Saying 'Aloha' means you never have to say good-bye!"

PENELOPE DYAN

www.ingramcontent.com/pod-product-compliance
Ingram Content Group UK Ltd.
Pitfield, Milton Keynes, MK11 3LW, UK
UKHW060136240426
12048UKWH00002B/56